Where Has My Prayer Life Gone?

#JustTake5

Shaerica Laine

AUTHOR'S CONTACT INFO

Email:
shaericawrightministries@gmail.com

Main Website:
www.allthingshaerica.com

Facebook:
www.facebook.com/shaericawrightministries

Instagram:

www.instragram.com/shaericawrightministries

Introduction

This isn't just another book about prayer! I'm not attacking your prayer life or lack of one. I wrote this under the leading of The Holy Spirit. This book is for the believer, the called intercessor and even the chosen Prophet, like myself. This is to help you as God helped me when I felt like I couldn't pray anymore.

There were moments when life became too much, and if I'm honest - I didn't want to pray. You know those moments in life when you are praying for things not to fall apart, but they fall apart anyway! Those moments when you are doing everything you know to do right, but the more you prayed, the worse things got. Then there are those moments when prayer just becomes a religious chore to check off the to-do list as a good Christian.

If you can relate to any of these moments - this book is for you!

So, what is #JustTake5? #JustTake5 is what The Holy Spirit gave me one day to help me regain my footing in prayer. It helped me to destroy the religious format of praying that I had been taught and had boxed God into. The intent of #JustTake5 is to help you stay connected to God through prayer. Your prayer life will change after reading this book if you are intentional about it!

Prayer?

What is prayer?

Prayer is to the believer what breath is to life. It's essential! We're always free to come to God! We can tell Him all that's in our hearts! Not only does God hear us when we pray; He has pity for our sorrow! Not only does He answer; He shows up with magnified power, endowed with mercy, for and in our deliverance!

As believers, prayer is the first conversation we should have with God each day He blesses us to wake up. I don't know why we make prayer so hard. It's simple! It's a conversation with God that takes on different forms, but it occurs when we talk!

As believers, prayer is our most powerful weapon, yet it is our least used one! The bible declares in 1 Thessalonians 5:17 that we are to PRAY WITHOUT CEASING. Many of us have taken this scripture out of context and made it a religious routine. To cease means to bring something to an end. So, what does it mean to pray without ceasing? It means that I'm constantly interacting with God, in some form of communication daily.

For example, when I wake up and say, "Thank You Jesus!"- I just offered up a prayer of worship and thanksgiving. When I say or do the wrong thing and The Holy Spirit convicts me, and I ask God for His forgiveness, I just offered up a prayer of repentance. When one of my patients come in and they're having a bad day, and I say a prayer for them in my head or out loud as The Holy Spirit leads, I just offered up a prayer of intercession!

In Exodus 33:11, the bible declares that the Lord would speak to Moses face to face, as one speaks to a friend. I don't think I can define prayer any simpler than this. Prayer isn't hard. If you can open your mouth, you can pray! If you can think, you can pray! If you can write, you can pray!

Are you ready?

Let's #JustTake5!

Father, You are amazing! There is nobody like You in heaven or earth! You are worthy of all honor and glory! Thank You for what You have done, are doing, and will do through this movement in the earth! Father, I pray that You would forgive me for my sins! Create in me a clean heart and renew the right spirit within me! I want Your glory in this book and Your favor to abound through prayer! Father, I pray for the vessel reading this book, I pray that every hindrance, distraction, excuse, limitation, and religious mindset be broken off their lives now in the name of Jesus! I decree and declare they have been loosed into a new place of grace to pray with power, authority, freedom, intimacy, and manifestation in Jesus Name! I decree, as they pray, their lives will never be the same, in the name of Jesus! God, I thank You for positioning us in a place of dominion to see, live, and be a part of Thy Kingdom coming and Thy will being done on earth as it is in heaven! Glory to our King, forever! In Jesus Name, Amen!

#JustTake5
Minute One
Enter In

Psalms 100:4 declares we are to enter His gates with thanksgiving, and into His courts with praise. Worship is the primary ingredient for a successful prayer life. I believe that many people struggle with prayer because they only have information about who they are praying to, instead of revelation of the One they are praying to.

When we learn to worship God, we prepare our minds and hearts for effective prayer. Worship and prayer cannot be separated. In order to pray, we must acknowledge The One we are praying to.

May I ask you a question? What do you believe about God?

Take a moment and write down what you know is true about God, not based on information but revelation. What does your faith say about God?

Hebrews 11:6 says, "And it is impossible to please God without faith. Anyone who wants to come to Him must believe that God exists and that He rewards those who sincerely seek Him." It takes faith to go to God, even in prayer. It takes another measure of faith to worship Him - not based on what we see (because what we see at times can be very discouraging) but solely on the divine truth of knowing who He is!

Did you write down those truths?

Now confess those truths with your mouth! I'll share as well!

God, You are so amazing! Father, there is no one like You! You are great and mighty. Your greatness is unsearchable! I love You, God! Thank You for being my healer, Jehovah Rapha. You are worthy, and nobody is deserving of the glory but You! You are my provider - Jehovah Jireh. My keeper, my sustainer, my deliver, and my counselor. I bless Your holy name, and I exalt Your name high above the earth. You are awesome! You are amazing! Glory to my God! How excellent is Your name!

I don't know about you, but I could go on and on describing my Daddy! I tell people all the time, "I don't know how to sing, but I know how to worship!" Worship is simply acknowledging who God is!

When Jesus gave us the format for praying the first thing He did, was worship God by acknowledging who He was - "Our Father who art in heaven, hallowed be thy name." (Matthew 6:9) I can imagine that you are saying, "Shaerica, you don't know what I'm going through or what I have been through and if I'm honest I don't feel like praying, let alone worshipping God!"

May I give you something that will set you free?

Worship isn't something we feel, it's what we are created to do! The fact is - no matter where we are in life, it doesn't change who God is!

In sickness and health, He is still Jehovah Rapha. In life and death, He is still Yahweh - I AM who I AM. With or without money, He still is Jehovah Jireh. And to the lost and saved, He is still Jesus!

When we mature in revelation of who God is, we desire to communicate (pray) with Him no matter what! Religion has taught us that worship is a formality during a service and only extends to when the praise and worship leader is before us.

I believe that King David can testify that through success and failures, God didn't change. David was RAW - a (Real. Anointed. Worshipper!) We all know of David's failures, yet the bible declared him by God's confession - a man after God's own heart. (1 Samuel 13:14)

I mentioned King David because many times we allow our failures to pull us away from God's presence.

What have you allowed to hinder you from pouring out on God?

Worship takes intimacy and getting over yourself! It takes crucifying the flesh daily and understanding that God owes us nothing but hell. Yet, we owe Him everything! It's a sacred place with Abba, our Father. Worship breeds intimacy.

Worship takes uncovering ourselves and removing the layers of self-righteousness because no one can approach God in that way. God wants us free in our approach to Him. The bible declares we can come humbly and boldly to the throne of grace! Did you know that when you can't find the right words to pray, there is power in your worship and praise?

Yes! It is called the prayer of praise and worship!

One of my favorite passages in the bible is that of Paul and Silas. Acts 16:16-34 NLT - "One day as we were going down to the place of prayer, we met a slave girl who had a spirit that enabled her to tell the future. She earned a lot of money for her masters by telling fortunes. "She followed Paul and the rest of us, shouting, "These men are servants of the Most High God, and they have come to tell you how to be saved." This went on day after day until Paul got so exasperated that he turned and said to the demon within her, "I command you in the name of Jesus Christ to come out of her." And instantly it left her. Her masters' hopes of wealth were now shattered, so they grabbed Paul and Silas and dragged them before the authorities at the marketplace. "The whole city is in an uproar because of these Jews!" they shouted to the city officials. "They are teaching customs that are illegal for us Romans to practice." A mob quickly formed against Paul and Silas, and the city officials ordered them stripped and beaten with wooden rods. They were severely beaten, and then they were thrown into prison. The jailer was ordered to make sure they didn't escape. So, the jailer put them into the inner dungeon and clamped their feet in the stocks. Around midnight Paul and Silas were praying and singing hymns to God, and the other prisoners were listening. Suddenly, there was a massive earthquake, and the prison was shaken to its foundations. All the doors immediately flew open, and the chains of every prisoner fell off! The jailer woke up to see the prison doors wide open. He assumed the prisoners had escaped, so he drew his sword to kill himself. But Paul shouted to him, "Stop! Don't kill yourself! We are all here!" The jailer called for lights and ran to the dungeon and fell down trembling before Paul and Silas. Then he brought them out and asked, "Sirs, what must I do to be saved?" They replied, "Believe in the Lord Jesus and you will be saved, along with everyone in your household." And they shared the word of the Lord with him and with all who lived in his household. Even at that hour of the night, the jailer cared for them and washed their wounds. Then he and everyone in his household were immediately baptized. He brought them into his house and set a meal before them, and he and his entire household rejoiced because they all believed in God."

Worship is the place where earth meets heaven! Bound and beaten, imprisoned due to no fault of their own - Paul and Silas did something amazing that shifted an entire prison! They prayed and sang hymns to God which caused heaven to erupt on earth! It didn't matter how they felt, what they were enduring, or what they saw! They seized the moment to lift worship to God. Because they got over themselves, mass deliverance and breakthrough happened not just for them, but those around them!

Every time we open our mouths, prostrate ourselves, and prepare our hearts to give God what is due to Him, we can expect a response! Therefore, the enemy works hard to keep us quiet because he knows the power in sound and words! That should shift something for someone!!

I don't know what you are facing or going through, but I dare you to OPEN YOUR MOUTH! Opening your mouth and giving God what is rightfully due to Him is the beginning of a powerful prayer life!

I have learned the power in the prayer of praise and worship! This is the place where I don't ask God for anything. I bless Him for who He is. And because He is good - He releases out of His kindness!

Now, let's put minute one into action! Make it personal!

Father, I give You praise, and I worship Your holy name. I ascribe to You the glory and honor that is due to You. You are my God! You alone are my Creator, my Lord and my Savior. You alone are deserving of my worship.

I worship You in the beauty of Your holiness. I bow down before You in reverent praise. You alone are worthy to receive all honor, glory, praise, blessing and worship. Your power and Your majesty are seen throughout all the world! The works of

Your hand are displayed in the heavens above, in the earth beneath and in the waters under the earth! You sit enthroned in the circle of the heavens as my eternal King. Your footstool is the foundation of the earth, which You have made! I am Your child. A sheep of Your pasture. You are my God and I worship You! You picked me up out of the miry clay and clothed me in Your own robe of righteousness. You cleansed me of my sins!

RIGHT HERE IS YOUR MOMENT TO KEEP PRESSING IN!!!!

_____

_____

_____

_____

_____

_____

_____

_____

_____

_____

_____

_____

_____

_____

_____

_____

#JustTake5
Minute 2
Repent

1 John 1:9 ESV states, "If we confess our sins, He is faithful and just to forgive us of our sins and to cleanse us from all unrighteousness."

Trying to get a prayer through with unconfessed sin, is like pouring liquid in a cup with a hole in it. It just falls to the ground. One of the greatest hindrances to a fruitful prayer life is sin! The bible tells us that when we approach God, we must believe who He is (Hebrews 11:6). Sincere worship should make us aware of who God is, and one thing is for sure - He is holy!

In Matthew chapter 6, Jesus taught His disciples how to pray. After Jesus acknowledged who God is, He taught them the importance of repentance saying to ask God to forgive our debts, as we forgive our debtors. If Jesus who was blameless approached the throne in humility, how much more should we approach the Father in this way, being full of sin. We should never think too highly of ourselves, regardless of how far God has brought us, we must remain humble. Every time I pray, I ask God for His forgiveness. Not because I am intentionally sinning, but because I need His grace and mercy daily.

Remember when I talked about David being a man after God's own heart. I truly believe David was deemed this by God because even in his failures, he didn't allow condemnation to keep him out of God's presence. He loved God's law and was quick to agree with God about his sin. When David messed up, he penned a beautiful letter recorded in Psalms 51.

"Have mercy on me, O God, because of your unfailing love. Because of your great compassion, blot out the stain of my sins. Wash me clean from my guilt. Purify me from my sin. For I recognize my rebellion; it haunts me day and night. Against you, and you alone, have I sinned; I have done what is evil in your sight. You will be proved right in what you say, and your judgment against me is just. For I was born a sinner yes, from the moment my mother conceived me. But you desire honesty from the womb, teaching me wisdom even there. Purify me from my sins, and I will be clean; wash me, and I will be whiter than snow. Oh, give me back my joy again; you have broken me now let me rejoice. Don't keep looking at my sins. Remove the stain of my guilt. Create in me a clean heart, O God. Renew a loyal spirit within me. Do not banish me from your presence, and don't take your Holy Spirit from me. Restore to me the joy of your salvation and make me willing to obey you. Then I will teach your ways to rebels, and they will return to you. Forgive me for shedding blood, O God who saves, then I will joyfully sing of your forgiveness. Unseal my lips, O Lord, that my mouth may praise you. You do not desire a sacrifice, or I would offer one. You do not want a burnt offering. The sacrifice you desire is a broken spirit. You will not reject a broken and repentant heart, O God. Look with favor on Zion and help her; rebuild the walls of Jerusalem. Then you will be pleased with sacrifices offered in the right spirit- with burnt offerings and whole burnt offerings. Then bulls will again be sacrificed on your altar."

When we come before God with sincere repentance, we experience the freedom of communing with our Father. David was a liar, manipulator, womanizer, adulterer, and murderer and God still loved him. And David didn't have Jesus like you and me! Wow! What a great revelation - knowing how much God loves us!

Take a moment and think about where you are in life right now. If you have any unconfessed sin, I want you to pause and #JustTake5! Praying a prayer of repentance or consecration is necessary in every believer's life.

When we are intentional to say this prayer, we invite God to change, rearrange, and purify us! Let's do it!

Father, thank You for being so loving and kind. I come before You humbly to ask for Your forgiveness. I make no excuses for (name the sin in your life). I know confession doesn't remove any consequences for my sin, but I thank You for the renewal in my confession. Father forgive me for the places I allowed sin to create distance between You and I.

Search me, oh God! Remove everything that's not like You and lead me into the way of the everlasting. Thank You for the blood of Jesus that has made atonement for my sins. In Jesus Name, Amen.

Now breathe! Inhale and exhale!

It feels so much better when you pray with freedom. A hindered prayer is a wasted prayer, and we don't have time to waste prayers!

Now that you have asked God for forgiveness, remember that you must also forgive! Jesus said to ask God to forgive us AS WE FORGIVE OUR DEBTORS! Forgiveness is a CHOICE. Many times, you won't feel it! That includes forgiving people who aren't apologetic to you!

I feel strength right here! The prayer wheel is turning! Holy Spirit - arrest every hindrance now in Jesus name! Holy Spirit - don't let the reader go any further in this book until they relinquish the root of unforgiveness operating in their life, in Jesus Name! I decree that the fire of God is consuming the shame, guilt, torment, and pride, in Jesus Name! We free ourselves from the rapist, molester, rejection, abandonment, divorce, loss, bitterness, devastation, eating disorders, depression, and oppression, in Jesus Name! Purge us God! Refine Us! Fix our hearts and minds, in Jesus Name! We leave nothing un-relinquished! Yes God! If it pulls You out of our

story or steals Your glory, we lay it at the altar now, in Jesus Name!

_____

_____

_____

_____

_____

_____

_____

_____

_____

_____

_____

_____

_____

_____

_____

_____

_____

_____

_____

_____

_____

_____

_____

#JustTake5
Minute Three
Don't Be Selfish - Pray For Someone Else

I believe one of the many reasons our prayer lives become stale, repetitious, and boring, is because we get hung up on ourselves too much. Don't get me wrong, there are times we have to go in for ourselves. However, there is a big difference in being repetitious in prayer versus being persistent in prayer.

Jesus is our great intercessor! He is constantly making intercession for us (Hebrews 7:25). Because He is always praying for us, He shows the importance of intercession. In Ezekiel 22:30, God was looking for someone to stand before Him on behalf of the land. God is always looking for someone to hear His voice and intervene on someone else's behalf.

We must understand that intercession is always prompted by the Holy Spirit. When we intercede for someone, we come to that persons' defense by speaking to God on their behalf. Have you ever felt that sudden urge to pray? Woke up out of your sleep at odd hours? Heard a name out of the blue or seen someone's' face? If you answered yes to any of these questions – then that is a burden of intercession you are feeling.

There is a power that is released when we intercede, and that is the power of the watchman and gatekeeper! In the natural, a gatekeeper is defined as someone who operates between the field officers and the chief. In addition, the gatekeeper is someone who controls access to something. We are given authority and access to act as legislators in the earth realm to see God's will fulfilled. When we intercede, we have the power to bind and loose according to Matthew 18:18.

Somebody needs your intercession! Pray them through in Jesus name!

I want to intercede for you now!

Father, thank You for the vessel reading this prayer right now. You are the Creator of every good thing. I know that You created the vessel reading this for purpose to fulfill destiny. Father, I ask You to forgive us of our sins. Create in us a clean heart and renew the right spirit within us. I come and stand as their intercessor and pray for this vessel that You have called Yours before the beginning of time!

I decree that every trouble in their life sent by the enemy is being crucified by the cross Jesus hung and died on. I call fourth the wind of God to blow fresh life into every dead place that was never supposed to die, in the name of Jesus.

I declare the peace of God is overwhelming them and removing frustration, anxiety, depression, and fear in Jesus name!

Father, I decree a newfound hope for this vessel according to Your word. God, You have promised to renew their strength, cause them to soar, to run and not be weary, to walk and not faint in the name of Jesus.

I decree they are experiencing newness now in the name of Jesus. I declare a new mind, new heart, and a renewed spirit in Jesus name.

I declare they are walking in the marvelous things of God.

Father, thank You that Your right hand and holy arm is upholding them and working for their good! I declare their present sufferings are not worthy to be compared to the glory You shall reveal in them. God, do a new thing in this vessels' life. Cause it to spring fourth now, in Jesus name! You make ways in the wilderness, and streams in the wasteland. I command new ways to spring forth in their life now in Jesus name!

I command new attitudes, new mind sets, new righteousness, new holiness, new commitment, and new submission. May they walk in the fulfillment You have ordained before time. Father, thank You for keeping this vessel. I believe You have kept them for such a time as this. I believe that You have a plan to prosper them, not to harm them, to give them hope and a future. Father preserve this vessel according to Your word.

I decree everything that is not in sync with Your heart for their life must be cast down, destroyed, and consumed by the fire of God, in Jesus name! Every dead weight must fall now, in Jesus name! Father make their path straight and cause this vessel to succeed.

Thank You for Your grace that is working now in their weak place, and Your strength that is showing Your great power. Father, I decree that the very thing they thought would break them is a catalyst for their destiny. God, I pray and believe that their life is changing in the name of Jesus! It is in the marvelous name of Jesus I decree these things shall be - for this vessel!

_____

_____

_____

_____

_____

_____

_____

_____

_____

_____

_____

_____

_____

_____

_____

_____

_____

_____

_____

_____

_____

_____

_____

_____

_____

_____

_____

_____

_____

_____

_____

_____

_____

_____

_____

_____

#JustTake5
Minute 4
It is Me Oh Lord, Standing In the Need of Prayer

Have you ever experienced being able to pray for everyone else, but struggled to find the words when it came to yourself? Trust me - you are not alone. I have experienced that plenty of times! As a matter of fact, I find it extremely easy to believe God for everyone - but me. I have seen God answer prayers that I've prayed for others so quickly; sometimes it blew my mind.

So, why do we struggle to find the words and faith for ourselves? May I offer you a few things that may help when you're standing in the need of prayer?

Consider the enemy within. It is easy to pray for others' needs, struggles, and blessings because we only fight on the surface for them. For ourselves, we must fight inwardly! When is the last time you took a good look in the mirror and made an honest assessment about your own character? Self-examination can be hard, because it means looking at your own sin.

Prayers for yourself do not have to be vague or selfish. They can be a tool for your sanctification. And God is glorified in your yielding. Remember the great Apostle Paul wrote in Romans 12:3,

"For by the grace given me I say to every one of you: Do not think of yourself more highly than you ought, but rather think of yourself with sober judgment, in accordance with the faith God has distributed to each of you."

Often, the real struggle is pride. May we remember to assess ourselves and go honestly, humbly, and boldly to the Throne of Grace!

Another reason we struggle is because we feel that it's selfish to pray for ourselves. Do you remember the story of Jesus before His crucifixion? If not, let me refresh your memory.

Matthew 26:36-46 NIV – *Then Jesus went with them to a place called Gethsemane, and he said to his disciples, "Sit here, while I go over there and pray." And taking with him Peter and the two sons of Zebedee, he began to be sorrowful and troubled. Then he said to them, "My soul is very sorrowful, even to death; remain here, and watch with me." And going a little farther he fell on his face and prayed, saying, "My Father, if it be possible, let this cup pass from me; nevertheless, not as I will, but as you will." And he came to the disciples and found them sleeping. And he said to Peter, "So, could you not watch with me one hour? Watch and pray that you may not enter into temptation. The spirit indeed is willing, but the flesh is weak." Again, for the second time, he went away and prayed, "My Father, if this cannot pass unless I drink it, your will be done." And again, he came and found them sleeping, for their eyes were heavy. So, leaving them again, he went away and prayed for the third time, saying the same words again. Then he came to the disciples and said to them, "Sleep and take your rest later on. See, the hour is at hand, and the Son of Man is betrayed into the hands of sinners. Rise, let us be going; see, my betrayer is at hand."*

Jesus was a man of prayer. There are recorded accounts of Him praying for many. He still intercedes for us today at the right hand of the Father. As much as Jesus was God, He was still man, and He took a moment to pray for Himself. In this text, Jesus was in a pivotal moment. He was in so much agony that He prayed three times for Himself.

Jesus teaches us that in times of suffering, it is okay to be selfish. He shows us full dependency on the Father and obedience unto death. I don't know about you, but if Jesus prayed for a way out - surely, we can too. I encourage you to get selfish about you - especially concerning prayer.

Our place of power is in prayer! The most powerful people are praying people! A closed mouth will not get fed! What is it that you have need of? Will God *not* provide every one of your needs according to His riches and glory (Philippians 4:19)? What do you want? Does God *not* grant the desires of your heart (Psalm 37:4)?

I encourage you to use the space below - on one side write your needs and on the other side write your desires (wants). Find scripture that agrees with what you need and want and pray that scripture out loud. Date these prayers, so when God answers, (He will answer), you can look back on this and rejoice at an answered prayer that you prayed for YOU!

Use the additional space below to write out prayers just for YOU! Are you ready? #JustTake5

_____

_____

_____

_____

_____

_____

_____

_____

_____

_____

_____

_____

_____

_____

_____

_____

_____

_____

#JustTake5
Minute Five
Give Him Glory

This is the place that you let hell know that no matter what you see - you trust God! I always seal my prayers with praise! I have learned the power of the benediction. There is approval, sanction, and blessing in the benediction!

Merriam Webster defines benediction, from its Greek roots the bene root is joined by another Latin root, dictio, "speaking." So, the meaning becomes something like "well-wishing." Perhaps the best-known benediction is the so-called Aaronic Benediction from the Bible, which begins, "May the Lord bless you and keep you."

When you bless God and give Him glory, you give heaven permission to access earth to BLESS YOU AND KEEP YOU! It is written in Colossians 4:2 KJV - ***Continue in prayer and watch in the same with thanksgiving!***

You have 60 seconds to bless Him good, like you know, that you know, that you know - JESUS DID IT! OH YES, HE DID!

Are you ready? #JustTake5!

Something Shifted

When God shifts us, there is an elevation that takes place! God will elevate **who** we are, to line up with the expected end He has for us. In order to access the next dimension, an exchange must happen. The wrong mindset, attitude and beliefs, will keep us stuck in our comfort zones, when God is trying to stretch us to make room for more and new.

I have learned to never get comfortable with what I see, because what I see does not always line up with what I know! Whatever season you're in right now - embrace it! Never let your belief of who God is, be predicated on what He does! Be encouraged and embrace this new dimension!

I prophesy a new mantle of intercession over your life in Jesus Name! I love you! I pray you have been blessed by this simple but powerful tool the Holy Spirit gave me in my hardest moments!

Remember a praying person is a powerful person!

Day 1
Prayer Time

Say This Prayer:

Dear Heavenly Father, thank You for loving me past my faults. I believe Your Word! I declare and decree that I am no longer living in my past! I decree I am restored, confirmed, strengthen, and established by You. Thank You Lord, for being my redeemer! I recognize that it is by Your grace I am saved by faith. Thank You for the gift of restoration. I receive it in Jesus name!

Now Continue Your Own Prayer:

_____

_____

_____

_____

_____

_____

_____

_____

_____

_____

_____

_____

_____

Day 2
Prayer Time

Say This Prayer:

O Gracious God - thank You for the freedom You have given me in Christ Jesus. I repent and confess all my sins, knowing that You are faithful and just to forgive me! Lord, save me from myself. I don't want to be in darkness any longer. I ask You to bring me into Your marvelous light. I decree - I am coming out of bondage and into freedom, in Jesus name!

Now Continue Your Own Prayer:

_____

_____

_____

_____

_____

_____

_____

_____

_____

_____

_____

_____

_____

Day 3
Prayer Time

Say This Prayer:

Father, thank You for fearfully and wonderfully creating me! Thank You for the price You paid for me so that I could be worth something. Father, I know I could never repay You for the price You've paid for me. Help me to walk in a manner that is worthy of the calling You have called me to. I am a virtuous child of the living God and I decree - I know my worth, in Jesus name!

Now Continue Your Own Prayer:

_____

_____

_____

_____

_____

_____

_____

_____

_____

_____

_____

_____

_____

Day 4
Prayer Time

Say This Prayer:

Father, thank You for life. You are the giver and taker of life. There is no one else like the Sovereign God I serve. Thank You for sending Your beloved Son to die for me. You have promised me that I can be of good cheer because You have already overcome depression, suicide, and death. I decree I will live abundantly, in Jesus name.

Now Continue Your Own Prayer:

_____

_____

_____

_____

_____

_____

_____

_____

_____

_____

_____

_____

_____

_____

Day 5
Prayer Time

Say This Prayer:

Father, in the name of Jesus, I humbly thank You for being my hope.
It is in You that I place my trust. I cast down every spirit of
insecurity, doubt, fear, unbelief, and worry at Your feet in Jesus
name. I have a renewed mind and I declare perfect peace, in Jesus
name!

Now Continue Your Own Prayer:

_____

_____

_____

_____

_____

_____

_____

_____

_____

_____

_____

_____

_____

Day 6
Prayer Time

Say This Prayer:

Father, in the name of Jesus, I humbly ask You to make me willing to obey! I surrender every place that has exalted itself above You in my life. Father lead me as I acknowledge You! I put my hope in You. I trust Your plan for my life! Help me to walk in the fullness of Jeremiah 29:11, in Jesus name!

Now Continue Your Own Prayer:

_____

_____

_____

_____

_____

_____

_____

_____

_____

_____

_____

_____

_____

_____

Day 7
Prayer Time

Say This Prayer:

Lord, thank You for the opportunity to serve in Your Kingdom. I decree I am fit and ready to serve in the KINGS' PALACE! I cancel every spirit of fear, doubt, defeat, and insecurity in Jesus name! I die to myself and take up my cross to bear and bring You glory. Thank You for my now time! I am walking into my season of now, in Jesus name!

Now Continue Your Own Prayer:

_____

_____

_____

_____

_____

_____

_____

_____

_____

_____

_____

_____

_____

_____

_____

Day 8
Prayer Time

Say This Prayer:

Lord, thank You for Your spirit that is everywhere I go. In everything I do, and everything that I am faced with - You are there. Lord, I pray that You would guide me in everything. Lord, when I feel alone, frustrated, hurt, and confused - help me to wait on You for direction so that I will not make the wrong decision. Father lead me into the way of the everlasting. Help me to take my eyes off man and put my eyes on You. Help me so that I won't allow someone else's sin to affect my thoughts. Help me to fully understand that we are all sinners saved by grace. The same grace You covered me therein, cover my brothers and my sisters until they walk in the light of Your truth. Have mercy on us, oh Lord, according to Your love and kindness, in Jesus name!

Now Continue Your Own Prayer:

Day 9
Prayer Time

Say This Prayer:

Father, thank You for the birthing process that allows me to birth something new. Lord, I ask You to give me strength and patience as I go through in Jesus name! Teach me perseverance that will produce character and character that will bring hope. My hope is in You. I know You will not disappoint me, and there will be glory after this, in Jesus name!

Now Continue Your Own Prayer:

_____

_____

_____

_____

_____

_____

_____

_____

_____

_____

_____

_____

_____

Day 10
Prayer Time

Say This Prayer:

Father, my prayer is simple. It is Your Word in Psalm 141:3. Set a guard O Lord over my mouth; keep watch over the door of my lips. Lord, help me to wait on You to be God. Lord, bridle my tongue when I want to speak but You have ordered me to be silent, in Jesus name!

Now Continue Your Own Prayer:

_____

_____

_____

_____

_____

_____

_____

_____

_____

_____

_____

_____

_____

_____

Day 11
Prayer Time

Say This Prayer:

Father, thank You for being so loving and kind towards me. Lord, I ask You to help me to deal with my inner self. Everything that offends You and others, I ask You to help me remove it in Jesus' name. I want to be a useful vessel, making impact for Your glory, in Jesus name!

Now Continue Your Own Prayer:

_____

_____

_____

_____

_____

_____

_____

_____

_____

_____

_____

_____

_____

_____

_____

Day 12
Prayer Time

Say This Prayer:

Lord, thank You for seeing about me in my grave condition. Lord, I receive Your resurrection power. I believe by faith that I have been raised out of my condition. I decree - whatever has held me bound, has to loose me and let me go now - in Jesus name! I am better, I have better, and I will do better, in Jesus name!

Now Continue Your Own Prayer:

_____

_____

_____

_____

_____

_____

_____

_____

_____

_____

_____

_____

_____

_____

Day 13
Prayer Time

Say This Prayer:

Lord, thank You for Your love that conquers all that I am and all that I face. Lord, I pray that You would heal me and give me peace in every area of my life. Lord, deliver me from dysfunctional relationships. Help me to develop the right relationship with You. I know by faith all other relationships will follow, in Jesus name!

Now Continue Your Own Prayer:

_____

_____

_____

_____

_____

_____

_____

_____

_____

_____

_____

_____

_____

_____

Day 14
Prayer Time

Say This Prayer:

Father, thank You for Jesus - Your Son, who is my Redeemer. Lord, I confess and repent of all sin; on all sides of my family. I break all ties, bonds, cords, and soul ties with all sin inherited from generational curses. Lord, I ask You to cleanse me and my family from all unrighteousness in Jesus name. I believe, receive, and decree - from this day forward, I am free from all things according to Your word in Acts 13:39, in Jesus name!

Now Continue Your Own Prayer:

_____

_____

_____

_____

_____

_____

_____

_____

_____

_____

_____

_____

_____

Day 15
Prayer Time

Say This Prayer:

Father, thank You for giving me a way to commune with You. I
know all I have to do is ask for Your help and You will be there for
me. I have confidence to know that if I ask You anything according
to Your will, You will hear me; anything I ask, will be granted. Father
give me a new desire to pray and let my prayers be effective, in Jesus
name!

Now Continue Your Own Prayer:

_____

_____

_____

_____

_____

_____

_____

_____

_____

_____

_____

_____

_____

Day 16
Prayer Time

Say This Prayer:

Lord, thank You for vision and purpose. Guide me through the process and keep me humble. Thank You Lord, for open doors, great success and new perspectives. Thank you for unseen provisions and connections that will create productivity in my life. I believe that You know my seasons and You are fully able to prepare me for all good things. Thank You that I walk in faith, believing wholeheartedly that my best is yet to come, in Jesus name!

Now Continue Your Own Prayer:

_____

_____

_____

_____

_____

_____

_____

_____

_____

_____

_____

_____

_____

Day 17
Prayer Time

Say This Prayer:

Father, thank you that all things work for my good! I know You have a plan for me. I receive my newness of life. I am waiting on my set place. You will produce patience in me that will have her perfect work. I will be steadfast, unmovable, always abounding in Your work. I know that I am being revamped, and my labor shall not be in vain, in Jesus name!

Now Continue Your Own Prayer:

_____

_____

_____

_____

_____

_____

_____

_____

_____

_____

_____

_____

_____

_____

Day 18
Prayer Time

Say This Prayer:

Lord, help me to find purpose in my broken place. Your Word says that it is good for me that I am afflicted, so I may learn your statues. Father teach me all You want me to know about You, and myself. I am more than a conqueror, in Jesus name!

Now Continue Your Own Prayer:

Day 19
Prayer Time

Say This Prayer:

Lord, thank You for looking beyond all my failures and mistakes. In spite of them, You still have need of me. Lord, I surrender all and give the will of my life to You. It all belongs to You. My eyes are open to see and my ears open to hear. Lord, I am ready to do what You have commanded me to do. I will be an obedient vessel, willing and useful for the Masters' purpose. I give You a new yes today. Lord, teach me to be comfortable as You deliver me, shape me, make me, and mold me into all You desire me to be. My life is not my own. I commit my whole life to You, in Jesus name!

Now Continue Your Own Prayer:

_____

_____

_____

_____

_____

_____

_____

_____

_____

_____

_____

_____

Day 20
Prayer Time

Say This Prayer:

God, thank You for making the announcement about me before You put me in my mother's womb. I make the bold declaration by FAITH - I am everything You have said about me - NOW! I'm not waiting to be; I am already what You have spoken!

I am equipped for every good work. The Spirit of The Lord is upon me to do the great work You have created me for! I decree by faith - nothing will detour or distract me from my Kingdom mandate. I will fulfill my purpose in the earth!

Finish this prayer with your own decrees. Walk Heavy, In Jesus Name!

Now Continue Your Own Prayer:

_____

_____

_____

_____

_____

_____

_____

_____

_____

_____

SHIFT HAPPENS AGAIN

Joel 2:32 declares that whosoever calls on the name of the Lord shall be saved.

God is faithful.

I declare a refreshing over your life in Jesus name. Fresh healing, deliverance, anointing, and fresh glory come to you now in Jesus name. The time is now for you to come out of Egypt! Release the old, so you may have the new.

Are you ready to walk away from the things that offend God? Don't assassinate your purpose or willfully abort His plan for your life any longer.

You have been delivered and called out for purpose.

In Jesus Name!

ABOUT THE AUTHOR

Pastor Shaerica Laine Wright is also gifted to the body of Christ as a Prophet and Evangelist. She is a lover of God and the people of God! She is a mother to three beautiful girls. She is a licensed and ordained minister of the Gospel of Jesus Christ. Shaerica is the proud Pastor of Divine Grace Ministries Int'l, Louisiana Campus. Pastor Shaerica is actively serving in her role under the covering of Apostle LaTrice Williams, Sr. Pastor of Divine Grace Ministries International. She is the founder and CEO of Shaerica Wright Ministries, a ministry in which she is dedicated to helping women from all walks of life understand their worth in Jesus Christ!

Pastor Shaerica has a passion for winning souls for Christ. She believes in standing as a watchman in prayer for the will of God to manifest in the earth. She released her first prayer CD in October of 2012 entitled "Travail With Me: A Prophetic Declaration of Prayers." She released her first book, "The Truth Set Me Free," in October of 2014. In January 2017, God opened a door for Pastor Shaerica to tell her story to over a million people by television. She appeared on CBN 700 Club. After her story aired, she was told by producers, over 200 people called in to give and rededicate their lives to Christ.

Known and loved for her powerful, prophetic preaching and teaching, Pastor Shaerica can be heard weekly imparting a word from God and interceding during her weekly Bible Study and Worship Services. Because of the way God has used her and her complete transparency when ministering, her name continues to be called to share in the spreading of God's great Gospel. For that, she is forever grateful and humbled by His grace.

Pastor Shaerica believes in being a virtuous woman according to Proverbs 31:10. She strives to walk in a manner that is worthy of her calling.

Pastor Shaerica lives by her motto - she is who she is today because she realized that she was nothing without God. It is in God she lives, moves and has her being!